Matters of the Heart

Written By

Sharon Jones

Faith by Grace Publishing

First Edition

Published by Faith by Grace Publishing

First Faith by Grace Publishing Printing 2014.

ISBN-13: 978-0692246894
ISBN-10: 0692246894

A record of the Library of Congress serial number can be acquired from the publisher.

Manufactured in the United States of America

Book layout and design by Ashlea Burns

Preface

Reflect back into the past, do you see then what you see now? Or is there a cloud of what used to be? How many times are we going through life holding on to the past still seeing clearly the hurts and pains, re-living our heart breaks, our fears, our tears. People may say it's just life but I'm here to say it could be "Matters of the Heart" that aren't meant to be forgotten or tossed away.

Dedicated to my loving husband for supporting me in everything I do, for encouraging me to write and for my daughter for helping me put this book together and showing me through writing her own books, that I can do it. To my beautiful grandchildren, children and my mom. I want to thank God for giving me the words to say, to be able to put this on paper for others to read, I pray that something in this book may help someone who is going through stuff in their lives, and I pray that God can speak to hearts. God bless.

Table of Contents

Chapter 1: Looking Back

The night was still, so quiet you could hear a pin drop as I stood there in the doorway of that small cabin that was tucked away between those beautiful mountains, so far off the road you had to have a four wheeler to get to it.

I opened the screen door and stepped out on to the porch, the beautiful view was breath taking. I could feel a soft warm breeze on my cheeks and feel my hair slightly blowing from my face. I looked up at the moon; it was bright, yet subtle as it beamed down at me. I smiled to myself and softly whispered "beautiful "as my thoughts went back to the times my husband and I sat outside our home and stared at the moon and stars, just talking and dreaming about life and how we were so lucky to find one another.

That was 38 years ago. Since then the world has

changed from decade to decade, some for better, some for worse. We struggled through bad times and rejoiced through the good ones. We watched as things slowly changed and looked forward to what the future held. Children were being born smarter than the generation before them, and technology was taking our jobs, but there must be change in order for the world to continue. It's such a slow progress, as test are ran and studies are made, there are failures but more accomplishments than not.

I sat on the steps and I just listened to the silence. Relaxing as I heard the crickets chirp in the distance, then the frogs began to croak, just as softly as if they knew, I just needed peace and quiet, just for a few days. That's why we came here, to just relax, rest our minds, bodies and souls, to spend time together and enjoy ourselves. Then I looked up to the heavens and Thanked God for everything, the good and bad that has matured us and taught us how to accept ourselves as well as to accept change as it comes.

Those few days of solitude was heavenly bliss and the nights were absolutely serene, that I just couldn't let my mind think of anything that was awaiting us when we got back home. I know God has everything under control, but it just seems like in the hustle and bustle of every day life, there just isn't any time to relax, even if you do have time to relax the body, then your mind never seems to stop, there is no turn off switch for it, the only peace that you can get, I mean real serenity is when you can rest within God, but its so hard to just be still and let the peace of God that surpasses any understanding submerge you.

The peace of God is what I need right now it seems

everywhere I turn there's someone there to bring me down with stories they have heard and they just take it and run, while I have to fight with the battles, to do and say things that are right. I struggle with what I shouldn't say or do, It's only natural to defend yourself but when you do, It usually ends up with putting another person down that has taken the words they have heard whether truth or not and ran with them just to have something to look good about. All that keeps going through my mind is that it's not my place to avenge myself, although sometimes it makes me feel better to set the record straight, other times it just makes me feel worse that I even said anything at all. When will I learn to just let God take care of it? That's a difficult thing to do.

Sometimes you just have to walk away from people whether it is family or friends because they refuse to see their wrong doings. They're so caught up in their own selfishness and think everyone owes them life. Yes, to be Godly about it you have to pray for them because it's the right thing to do but realize they don't see anything they do as wrong, they just please their flesh by running their mouths and being instruments of Satan. Sometimes walking away means you don't invite them into your home or you block them on social media's such as Facebook even if they are family because some people have no conception of how they are Satan's instruments. They're jealous and don't know how to deal with it and they have no appreciation or respect for anyone or anything. But you can have peace like nobody's business because they have no idea what is headed their way.

God is on your side if you do things like he tells you to. That's the way others will treat you, it may not be from the same people you prayed for and let things go with but it will come back to you in good. Which means they will get treated the same way they treated others. Sometimes that's the only way people learn anything.

God has brought us through many difficult times. He's been our strength in times of weaknesses, he's been our shield that sharpened the blows, and He's been our refuge, our Rock. Without Him, I have no idea where I might be Today. I'm so glad that He never left me, even when I didn't deserve it, he still loved me and held on to me, whispering to my soul, with compassion and love, as he continued to lead me down the path to His abode where he is teaching me to Spread my wings to fly.

Chapter 2: Heartache

As I write this, my mind wonders back to some events that shows how strong one can be, beginning with my grandchildren and how something's will always remain in your heart.

It was a cold January night, as I stood on the porch looking up at the stars, they were brightly piercing through the somewhat cloudy sky, the trees were bare, their branches gently blowing in the light breeze. I looked up to the Heavens; as thoughts bombarded my mind and my heart begin to break all over again.

I shivered as my mind was taken back to that day 9 years ago when we stood at the cemetery, on the hillside, in back of a small country church, my son and daughter-in-law had lost their only son, to birth defects, and as the song "Will the circle be unbroken" was played so sweet and mellow on the banjo by my son, and the words asked the undertaker to please drive slow, no one wanted to let go of the precious little angel, but there was no choice, at least in the physical realm, but spiritually even until today he still lives in our hearts.

My heart shattered into a million pieces as I held him in my arms that day at the hospital, in that little room, he was wrapped in a blanket and as I put my face against his sweet little angelic face, my tears covered his face, and was sent to heaven with him, God saw those tears and he has brought us through, as he has so many times before, but does the heart really completely heal?

I wonder sometimes as I watch my son seem to punish himself with self inflicted pain, as he pursues his wrestling career. My heart cries out to "God Almighty" to heal his heart with each passing day.

My daughter-in-law, I don't see much anymore but I know she still feels the pain as they both try to close this chapter of their lives with some assurance that this is just a part of life, since that day when Adam and Eve chose to eat of the forbidden fruit in the "Garden of Eden" so many years ago. Also, I know they will see him again one day, if they have put their trust in The Lord Jesus Christ.

God allowed them to spend 4 months with that little one. Which I am sure they cherish through out the passing years, even if they only got to hold him periodically through that time, they sat there every minute they possibly could, right by his side, only leaving when they had to and in those days they loved that little guy with every drop of love they had in their being and no matter how many years pass he will remain in their heart until that day when they're reunited.

I was jolted back to reality as a gust of cold air hit me in the face, I looked back to the stars thinking, each star is one of the angels, God chose to be with Him. My dad, my mom, grandparents, my sister, aunts and uncles, each shining down on us.

I smiled as my thoughts drifted back to memories of each one and I thanked God for the time he gave me with each of them, my little grandson being the shortest time, Then there are the 4 miscarriages my daughter has gone through, although we never met the little ones they still remain in our thoughts and hearts, they were very much alive as they struggled for survival in their mother's womb, again I have to ask, does the heart ever really completely heal? I often wonder who they are and why they were chosen to go be with God even before they took their first breath in this World, thoughts of how special they are to live with God, fill my heart and mind.

We all have loved ones who are waiting in the land beyond the sky to welcome us into the

Kingdom of God when our time comes to say goodbye to the heartaches, the pain, the disappointments, the turmoil of this sin filled world.

But for now, we travel on in this journey, doing things we need to do to survive, Helping others along the way, living life sometimes the way we choose, other times the way God chooses, but ultimately He is our maker and to Him and only Him will we stand before one day to be judged and sent to our eternal destination.

Isn't it awesome that God so Loved the world that he gave his only sons' life so that we may live? I have to thank him every day for a chance to see His creation and meet others he has chosen to walk this journey with me.

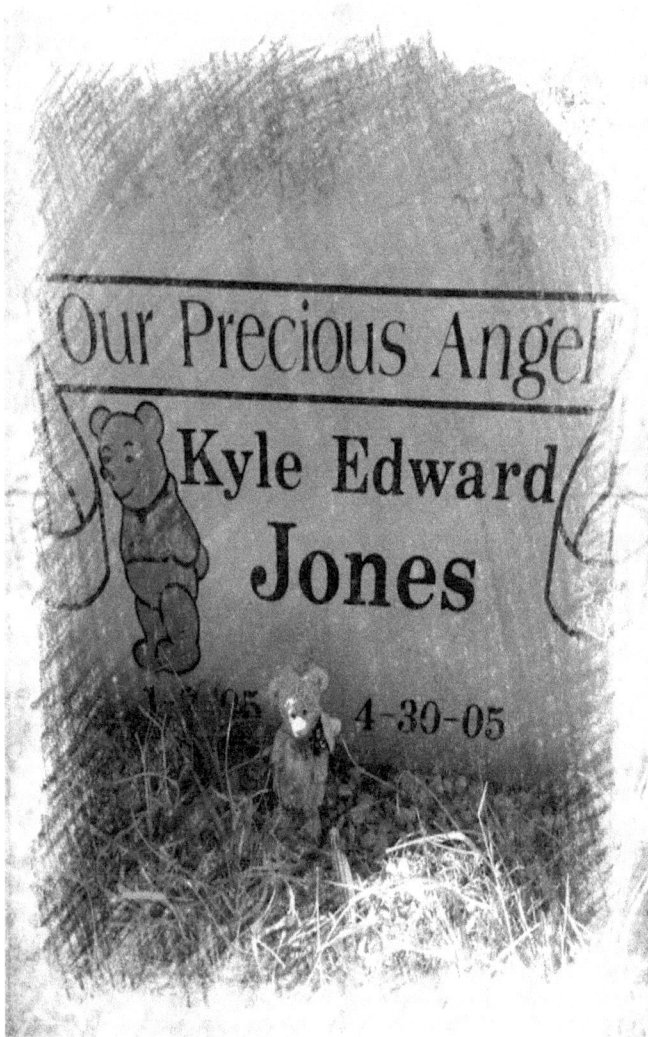

Our Precious Angel

Kyle Edward Jones

1-?-05   4-30-05

Chapter 3: Reminiscing

I went in the house and I looked for David, my husband of 38 years, He was my high school sweetheart, he had just came through a brutal surgery on his shoulder and was recouping at home a few weeks. I found him in his favorite recliner, laid back relaxing, watching some TV. When he saw me he smiled, asking me what I was doing.

"I was just out star gazing" I replied to him.

"What did you see?" he asked. "Your face is glowing." He said, as I   began to tell.

I smiled "I love my visits with my love ones and with God." I replied. He kissed my head and gave me a hug and went back to watching his show.

This was one of the many times he has had surgery. In 1995 he had a back surgery that was supposed to be 5 hours, but ended up in a 14-hour surgery and several days in intensive care.

In the last couple years he's had heart surgery, gallbladder and knee surgery and now this, but he still does what he has to do to make it, He's one of the strongest people I know. He has stood by me, through thick and thin and he would give you the shirt off his back. He at one time was taking care of me and my mom, taking us both back and forth to doctor appointments, cooking our meals and doing stuff for us we couldn't do for ourselves, while healing from gallbladder surgery, I'm not talking about the microscopic surgery where there's a small incision and a couple holes, I'm talking about cut from under his breast all the way down the side of his belly where he had to be cut because his gallbladder ruptured. He was with me by my mom's side, holding her hand when she took her last breath, leaving this world behind; she entered into Gods arms as he welcomed this angel home.

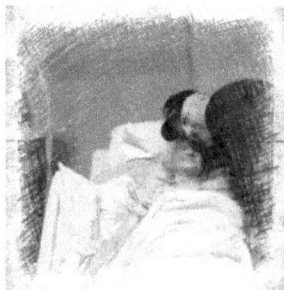

I'm sure she has every one of those beautiful grand babies in her arms, playing with them even as I speak and as you read this.

I remember when David and I first met, I was so shy, I wouldn't even speak, and although when I got past him I would smile to myself. After that, everywhere I turned at school he was there, slowly I began to smile at him, and then speak to him still blushing every time I was near him. Then the day came when he asked me to the basketball game in the gym, we sat there close watching the game, and then as we were about to leave to go catch the bus, he stopped and looked down at me and he kissed me, my head was spinning and I smiled all the way home as I looked out the back window to see if I could catch a glimpse of him on his bus. That was my first experience of true love.

We married in October 1975 and we started our life together. Three years passed, then our son was born, nothing can describe the feeling of having a little human being laid in your arms for the first time. Three times God blessed us with our children, two sons and a daughter and I thank God for each of them every day.

The years seem to pass by so quickly as we raised our children. They've all grown into strong reliable adults, they've each chosen their paths in life and I'm very proud of each one, they all go out and chase their dreams, they don't just sit and wait for life and dreams to come to them and my daughter should know that I started writing years ago mostly writing poems, tucked away In a little book on the shelf, then one day I put them in my computer and saved them. I had written other stuff to help people and myself too, but over the years I pretty much forgot about the writings, even though I had a poem published. I thought that was as far as it went. Until a couple years ago I started two writings and saved them on my computer, then a few weeks ago I just had that urging to write but couldn't, So I played around with the stuff I had written and started putting it together with my poems and decided to let her and David read them, I knew after their reaction that it was time to put it to print and thanks to my daughter writing her own books, and having them published I could take this step into the future. Up until my husband and I took our three kids to church back when my daughter was born, I thought life was complete, until we went to church one Sunday and as we stood there listening to the preaching and listening to the music something happened on the inside as my husband and I stood there we both looked at each other, we made our way to the front of the church and accepted

Christ into our lives. Now that really did make life complete.

We were blind to the difficulties and trials to come but here I am today, years later and still believing in the one who even made this life possible.

Do I regret things that I've done and said or for those matter things I haven't done or said also. The answer is yes, very much so.

I know the road is becoming very short now, that any day Our Savior will be calling all his children home to live with Him forever.

While that makes me happy and I want to rejoice I still feel sad in my heart for those who've never experienced God in their lives or have, but somehow has gotten off track and can't find the way back through grief, pain, mental illness etc. and many other ways. But what can I do, I'm one person, often struggling just to keep my head above water, spiritually, physically, mentally etc. People say you can pray, yes I can, if I could, sometimes my own life and what it brings is so overwhelming that I can't do anything and sometimes what I do, or say is wrong, The only thing I do know is that God is the one who can change things no matter what it is or isn't. So I do what I can and I trust God to do the rest.

Our 3 children are all grown now and have families of their own, what a blessing those grandchildren are. Our son who lost their little one to birth defect is now remarried and a proud father of a 5yr old daughter, she'll be raised to know that she has a little brother in heaven,

Our oldest son and his wife have a boy and a girl who are teenagers now and we love seeing them growing into such strong well-grounded, young adults. Our daughter has a 6 year old girl and two boys ages 4 and 2, and boy, those babies keep us young. It amazes me how smart these little ones are, how their little minds absorb stuff said and done like a sponge. They can be funny at times and believe me there is never a dull moment around them.

Christian my daughter's 2 year old, is the only grand child my mom didn't get to see, at least here on this earth but maybe she seen him in that other world as he passed from there "The gift from God to birth". My daughter was pregnant with him when my mom passed. She would have loved him so much; he's such a loving little one. I'm not sure if the 4 year old remembers her or not but he was a joy to her in her last few days. He would make her smile when he was here. I guess since mom lived with my daughter awhile before she got sick and after, she got closer to them and just enjoyed watching them grow and learn.

Life can bring some unexpected things; we just need to remember we always have one who is in complete control when we have God in our lives.

"In Loving Memory
Kyle Edward Jo...
1/7/05-4/30/05

BLESS OUR LITTLE ANGEL

Chapter 4: Past & Present

My mother who was always healthy and walked several miles a day to and from work unexpectedly had a heart attack, she was rushed 200 miles away to a heart center. She was 76 years old and was given a 10% chance of coming through the surgery, which luckily she did, Thank God.

We sat by her bedside, my husband and I and our kids for 28 days, but then on the night before she was to get released from the hospital, they flew my sister in with a massive heart attack, she was in a comate state, to far gone to do surgery. She was sent to hospice, where she died one week later and as we prepared for the funeral service we were sad not knowing where she would spend eternity, but God gave me a song on the radio, that we played at her service, which said all we needed to hear and that was Sissy's song by Alan Jackson.

Through all this with my mother, my sisters and

brother seem to have their own things going on, offering very little help, Thank God for my husband and children and a couple aunts and uncles that came to our rescue, helping us with her until she got back on her feet, which was a slow process, she told me when she was in the hospital that I was her angel while she was there, said that I slept with her, when really I was in a waiting room or in our blazer or van and occasionally in a hotel room.

My mom took care of my dad for 8 years after he had a stroke and he died 21 years ago and although we expected him to go anytime it still wasn't easy after the 8 years, but like with mom God prepared us. My oldest son told me one time his grandfather saved his life when he was a fire fighter. He appeared to him in that burning building and guided him out. My children was kind of young when he passed but they spent enough time with him to love him very much and I'm sure he still remains in their hearts to this day.

Mom would witness to people and my dad couldn't get over it. He ended up giving his life to God in the last few years of his life because of her.

She would witness to my son-in-law who was a catholic boy all his life. She would tell him only God could forgive your sins, not man. He argued with her some but she got him and my daughter to go to the Pentecostal church of God where she was raised in and they both re-gave their lives to The Lord and a year later they began ministry in the church. Ashlea into the children's church and Patrick into the ministry where he's allowing God's anointing to flow through him. Mom would be so proud of both of them. My daughter has also pursued her writing, which was something that my mom and myself were really proud of her for working towards.

God was with her as he was with us strengthening us to go through it all. She lived for two years before God took her to be with him. God prepared us for his taking; he helped us accept that she was on her way to heaven. It was hard watching her take her last breath, but I think explaining it to my little granddaughter who was only 3 at the time, was just as hard.

I remember her being there when her "Granny Grace" as she called her, was sick. Mom would let her and the other grandchildren up in the bed with her sometimes. They seem to make her day. If they weren't there she would ask for them.

We would leave the room when mom was resting or sleeping even when the grandchildren was here and I remember Graci going to the door and looking in mom's room and mom was awake and little Graci shook her head and said to herself, but out loud enough for mom to hear. She said, "Nobody is watching Granny Grace." My mom was giggling, despite the pain she was in.

That little girl is just a special little girl my mom would say. My mom had mentioned to Graci that one day soon she may have to go sleep on a cloud because that's where mom kept telling us she was sleeping when she would sleep. She would tell her the bed was so hard because she had been in that bed for weeks.

The day my mom passed away we knew she was not going to make it and although my daughter and sons was there we didn't let the grandchildren come because they were to young to understand.

So the next day I was sitting in my mom's room working on some pictures of her, for her service and Graci came bouncing through the door and stopped in her tracks and had a really concerned Look on her face, then she looked at Mom's bed and then looked at me and asked, "Where is Granny Grace?" I sat there a second and I didn't know what to say.

Finally I said "She went to go sleep on a cloud for awhile because her bed was so hard."

I handed her a picture of my mom and a little plant mom had in her room and I said, "Granny Grace said to give you this." She took them and seemed to accept it. A little later she was outside blowing kisses up to the clouds to Granny Grace. It was just so hard seeing her hurting and even through the past couple years she still misses her Granny.

She just asked me recently if people get old like Granny Grace do they die?

And before I could answer she said, one day you will get old and die, everyone does, but I hope it will be a long time before you do and I told her that if I died I want her to know I will always love her and I would be waiting to see her again one day just as she will be able to see her Granny Grace one day.

She seemed ok with that but then later when I told her she had to go home after spending the night and day with me, she told me she was afraid one day she would come to my house to see me and I would be gone like Granny Grace. She is only 6 years old now and even at 3 it was a "Matter of the Heart" for her. So I really don't think there is an age thing there. Matters of the heart are for the young and old and aren't all meant to be forgotten. I think sometimes the memories are what help the heart to heal to a certain degree.

I am a child of God who has been chosen by Him to walk 54 years so far in this world, that He created, while there is sadness, wars and chaos and so much going on in this world, the ugliness, the sin and all the death and pain etc., This is still a world that God Almighty has created and it's a very beautiful place as well.

As I walk down the path to my destiny, I look

around and I see the beautiful mountains, the flowers and the trees, the ocean, the beautiful sunsets and all the beauty and I begin to Thank God for just life in such a beautiful place of His choice.

In a land where we have much more freedom than some other countries have, yet while enjoying my freedom I still pray for those in other countries, that they to may experience the same freedom. Regardless of that, we're still all Gods creations, uniquely made in His image and while some doesn't have the freedom we do. We all have the ultimate freedom provided by God Himself, even if there's no freedom in this world where you can worship pray and all, We still have the freedom in our hearts, nobody can take that away from us. So as you pray, Thank God that for freedom.

God's creations are the most awesome things on this earth, He gave it to us to enjoy, to sooth us and help us to regain our lot in life. When we sometimes lose our way or just grow tired and weary, just look at your surroundings, Reflect back into the past, do you see then what you see now? Or is there a cloud of what used to be? How many times are we going through life holding on to the past, still seeing clearly the hurts and pains, reliving our heart breaks, our fears, our tears. People may say it's just life, but I'm here to say it could be "*Matters of the Heart*" that aren't meant to be forgotten or tossed away.

My husband and I went to the beach and as I was sitting there watching the sunrises, hearing the ocean and thinking about how serene it was, my thoughts were also going to the people in Japan, a couple years ago a wave came through (forget how many miles long), destroying everything in its path, what a disaster, my heart goes out to the ones who have lost loved ones and who are still looking for their loved ones and to them for what they survived, what they went through and are still going through to survive now with their homes are destroyed and then the nuclear thing going on. All I can do is pray for them. Actually those are signs from God telling us His coming is upon us.

Even the USA may have the nuclear effects in our air soon, but for now we are moving very fast right into the beginning of a new era where sin is being pushed to the top priorities and salvation is being pushed to the bottom, even more so now than ever.

I for one find it so sickening how children and the elderly are being treated in this world and how homosexuality and racism etc. are being lifted up and made to seem that all the sudden that those things are of utmost importance, Christianity, morals and decency are put down, but that just proves all the more what I've been saying about the coming of The Lord.

We just have to pray, hang onto God and reach out to everyone we can, to let them know time is growing so short, and no matter what else we do, we have to Trust in God and except him as savior of the world, nobody is exempt, He sent His son Jesus to die for everyone's sins, but only if we confess and except him as our Lord and Savior will we be cleansed.

I say all this to say "Always trust in God", He knows best, he will never let you down, even though it may seem he does, we're not looking at the whole picture like he sees it. Never give up, always keep your eyes on the one who can and will bring you through anything and everything life sends your way.

Rejoice every day and Praise Him for all He was, is and will always be. Love the Lord with all your heart, forever and always.

Chapter 5: Poems

Written when my kids were little

To all the mothers out there, love your little ones every day, be patient and realize one day you can look back at so many thing they've done and see the art, from these messes and make memories in your heart.

"God Made Me To Do My Best"

I may be little
I may be small

But whatever I Do
I give my all

My little hands,
My little feet

Are both Gods tools
Made small and sweet

See my handprints on the walls
See my footprints too?

I tried to wash them off -
But I think they're on with glue

I wonder what my mom will say
When she sees this big mess

When all I can say to her
Is Mom I did my best

Written when I first began serving God

"Will you answer that knock and let Jesus come In?"

The lord was knocking at my hearts door

saying my child let me enter in

Saying do you know that you are living

for the master of all sin?

If you will just open the door from inside

and let me enter in

In me you can deeply confide

and be cleansed of all your sin

Believe that I died and suffered

and bled upon Calvary's tree

That my blood was painfully shed

so you could be set free

My blood will cover you from head to toe

on the inside and on the out

And in my grace you shall grow

and I will teach you what I'm all about

With these words I said unto him

believing as I knelt

Forgive me Lord of all my sin

let your love within me be felt

For I will welcome you into my heart
To dwell forever more
Thank you for a brand new start
For knocking at my hearts door
Salvation is as simple as this poem says,
if you don't know how to pray
And accept Jesus, just read these words.

-God bless-

"Jesus Reign"

When you accept Jesus within
Satan is then put out in the cold
There He must stay
Jesus help me to be bold
Jesus help me, I pray
As I journey down the path
Toward my heavenly home
Hold my hand and with me talk
Help me not to aimlessly roam
Or out of your will walk
And when I stumble and happen to fall
Pick me up and push me along
Teach me to listen when you call
Help me to do right from wrong
When trials are sent by my way
And life don't seem the same
Help me Lord I pray
To praise your Holy name
Teach me obedience, truth and trust
And how to shine for you
Show me Lord it is a must
To apply your word in everything I say and do
I pray Dear Lord that souls can be won
As I witness of your love
That they to will believe, in Gods one and only Son
And have a home prepared above
For the day is coming near

For the Heavenly Father to say
Tell my children not to fear
On that wonderful day
For life is not over, but only begun
When they hear the trumpet sound
Because they are the ones whose names are found
Written in the Book of Life
Where in heaven there will never be
Trouble, woe and strife
But we will all live in Eternity of Love
With our blessed Redeemer of sin
In a home far above
When we receive Jesus within

-Let Jesus reign-

"Written when my sister died" 3/28/09

"God looked down from heaven and he saw a rose"

God saw Kathy was very tired and weary from life's toll
He said it's time to bring her home
Her time there is 'or
The Holy Spirit interceded for her soul
Then he slowly opened heaven's door
He prepared her for his presence
And greeted her with a smile
Took her hands in his and embraced her heart so dear
He said I know that was rough, that last mile
But now you do not have anything to fear
For I am Your Savior, Your Lord, Your Friend
And here with me you will dwell forever more
Right there her heart began to mend
And the petals on that rose fell to the floor
A pure white rose stood in her place that day
She fell to her knees in awe at his presence so sweet
Reverence and praise was all that she could say
Then she said, it's You, my Lord
I have been waiting to meet
He touched her cheek and wiped away her tear
Said my child, you are my chosen one fair
I have taken away all the pain
And fear you are in my loving care
Reach out to God and give him your heart
And trust him in everything coming your way
Trust him for a brand new start
And for the Judgment Day

Written when my mom died

"Mommy Dearest"

The years went by and days became all the same
Yesterday's lost in the past
Tomorrow's fortune hardship
And fames came and went
But they did not last
But she had a good lived life
Reaching out to others in love
Reaching God in brand new height
Adorning the Father above
She experienced Gods Devine healings
All throughout her life with faith so strong
She never went by passive feelings
Because she knew to whom she belonged
Each one who knew her, knew the strong love
And loved her sweet, sweet smile
Sent through her from God above
Because she always went that extra mile
Now Momma Dearest Rest in Peace
Take in all God has for you
For in prayer you never did cease
Your loved ones will be born anew
So in Heaven one day very soon
We shall all meet again there
Maybe morning, night or noon
We will all be in His loving care
We love you Mom, so very much and we miss you
But we know you are in Heaven
Land of Healing and Devine love

Sitting in Jesus' lap
Wrapped in Devine love and healing
True looking down from heaven ,
That perfect place above
Thank you, Mom for your unconditional love
That flowed through you from Jesus the king
Look upon us from there above
And let us hear you sweetly sing
On the wings of a snow white dove
He is carrying you to your final rest
Symbol of Devine peace and love
You are in the arms of the best
I will see you in the stars at night
I will see you in the bright sunshine
Take care of my babies, until I see the light
And until heaven is also mine

By: Sharon Jones 2011

Written when baby Kyle passed away.

"Heaven is my home"

I am in Jesus arms
The angels carried me here
I look down and I can see no harms
I can see no earthly fear
But I can see sadness and pain
Upon each face I see
I know you feel sometimes insane
But all this for me?
Why do you cry and look away
When you see my eternal rest
I too remember that day
When Jesus said to me, I am his best
He sent his angels to get me
We all flew to home above
Wait until you get here to see
There is so much joy and love
I didn't want to leave you
But knew I couldn't stay
But I see all that you do
As I run, jump and play
Please prepare your soul to come here one day
Accept Jesus for a new start
All you have to do is pray
And you will receive a brand new heart

"In Loving Memory
Kyle Edward Jones
1/7/05-4/30/05

BLESS OUR LITTLE ANGEL

Written for my grandbabies in heaven

Our tiny angels, in heaven above
Where how and why
All questions out of love
As unto God we humbly cry

Only God knows why he took you
Before you became complete
In earthly form soul's anew
Souls we did not get to meet

Be a tiny being, in that spirit light
As I look into the sky above
I See the twinkle in the stars so bright
I see you looking down with God's love

Wait for us and be in God's care
Watching over you each day
Sometimes it's to much to bear
Lord God help us I pray

We will see you one day very soon
When God brings us to your side
Morning night or maybe noon
Together with him we all will all abide.

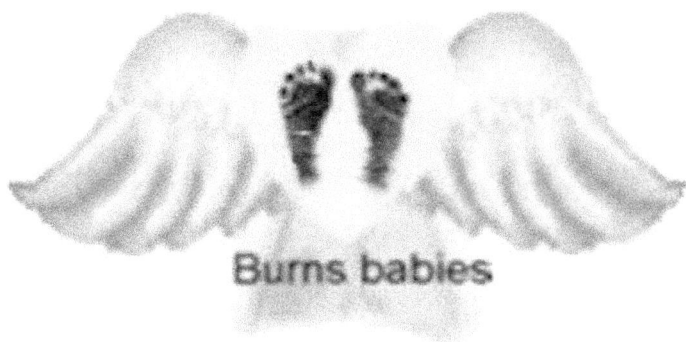

Burns babies

These poems were written throughout the years, and I included them in this book because they are matters of the heart.

"Receive Jesus and Live"

Jesus my Lord I want to know
Thee more and more every day
Make me Lord what you want me to be
To Thee Lord Jesus I pray
Guide me and keep me on the right track
Teach me to witness of You
Don't let me ever turn my back
Or anything out of your will do
There are souls lost in the darkness of sin
That Satan is holding on to with all his might
But with prayer and thankful praise for them
We as Gods children will win the fight
For the Lord is with us, as we speak unto them
About Jesus the cross and the blood that was shed
And how asking and believing will free us from all sin
And free us from that dying dread
Because when we accept Jesus from within
And be washed with His blood so pure
And put our full trust in Him
We can all patiently endure
When the time comes
When we are to leave out of this world
To a life of peace
Jesus will be standing with outstretched arms
To receive us from Satan's complete release

"Sinners Beware"

There are signs all over creation
That time is nearing an end
And we all need a relation
With someone, on whom we can depend
The one with all the power
Over all of these lands
The one that at this hour
Standing with outstretched hands
Just waiting for you to welcome him in
To reside in a temple of love
Waiting to cleanse you of all your sin
And prepare you a home in heaven above
For He created us one and all
From the dust of the ground
And when Adam and Eve sinned,
He saw Satan would know no bounds
As time went on and evil kept dwelling
God had Noah to build an ark, knowing
That man would not heed to the words spoken
A warning of destruction was near
But He gave a chance to all that would believe
That they would have no fear
When the Earth was to receive
Noah kept warning them destruction was near
A flood of water to destroy the sin
That Satan had so the land filled
A with a promise to this day, there has been
A rainbow in the sky revealed
The people would not listen to Satan even on that day
As he took the animals and his family into the ark

The people laughed saying no way
Until the skies were stormy and dark
But then it was to late
To enter the safety of the ark
Because Noah listened to God when he was warned
That destruction was about to abound
He didn't listen to the people's cries of scorn
As the water gushed over their heads
And they were drown
They were for a very long time warned
But they refused to heed where they were bound
Now not long after, sin again arose
Within people everywhere
And they rejected God who knows
For He was always there
Then an Angel of God was sent to the earth
To tell a certain woman, who God chose to be
As the mother of the savior, she would give birth
For all the world to see
Christ was born, in a manager he laid His head
Then He grew and taught the Words to believe
They came to hear Him and be fed
And His passion and Love they did receive
He was crucified on a cross, Bore all of our sin
As he cried out to The Father
And looked above denied by some who walked with Him
He forgave with all His Love
Now He awaits for you as He intercedes for all
To accept Him into your heart
All you have to do is upon His name call
And you will have a brand new start
Sinners beware of warnings from above

He knows all about the hearts,
That are yearning within
He's warning us out of His love
So believe and ask forgiveness of your sin

"Trust in Jesus and be a witness for him"

As time is wearing on day after day
I find myself wanting to go
And be with my Jesus
And hear him say you are the reason
I died on that tree
As I hung on that cross
I looked down through time
And saw all my children who believe in me
Satan making you feel it was a crime to trust in
me to set you free
But I am your lord, The Savior of all
And I'm always at your side
And upon me you can call with you
I will always abide
Satan will tell you Vie gone away
Because you stumbled and slipped
But you I will not betray
But your sins when asked,
Will be in my blood dipped
Covered and forgiven and remembered no more
When from your heart you confessed
You can be absolutely sure that I know what is
Best that's why I'm leaving you here longer
To witness to some of the ones
Who Satan to them seem stronger
Than gods only son
So when I send you to the lost
Remember that my blood was shed
To pay the price that it cost

And through my word you shall be fed
And you will know of how to do my will
For I have already began to make the lost feel
My presence and how i can lead them to love in
me
And to trust for forgiveness of their sin
And the light to see that I'm always with them
The day is coming very soon
That you can come to your heavenly place
To be with me without any more pain
To see me face to face
And for everlasting eternity you shall remain
So be patient and be of good cheer
Spread the gospel to all that will hear
You will have a reward waiting you
For each one you witnessed to
Your will not mine
Although I dont really understand
For what God wants for my life's will
He will take me by the hand
And help me not to go on how I feel
For he has so many things in store
That he will bring to pass
And Ill learn what they are for
And Ill know what of him to ask
To be in his will is my hearts desire
To know I'm pleasing him
For he picked me up out of the muck and mire
And washed away my sin
He suffered and bled upon Calvary's cross
So painful it must have been
All to assure I wouldn't be lost

In Satan's world of sin
Lord I surrender my will to your will
Of my life you have control
With my life you can deal
Take this clay and mold into whatever you desire
No matter what it may be put me in the roaring
fire
But just help me to see that there is a process of
Teaching and experiencing pain
All done by you with love
For my spirit you have to train
Lord the battle is not mine
When I surrender it unto you
I need peace of heart and mind
As I'm gong through this storm
As it rages more and more within me
Everything seems so foreign
Satan wont let go
As my strength seems to fade
To me I need Jesus to show
That satan cannot invade
Into my heart which belongs to the Lord
Although satan keeps pouring it on
I know I cannot afford
To let him make me think my lord is gone
Because deep within me I feel
The Lords presence as though he's near
And that this mountain is only a hill
And I will make it not to fear
But the more I think I see the rays of sunshine
Beneath the cloud satan has his knifing ways
Of shouting at me oh so loud
Saying forget it, your doomed to die

God isn't anywhere to be found
But I rebuke satan and I cry
I am heavenward bound
To receive eternal everlasting life
With my Jesus, the very one
Who will free me from all this strife
God's one and only son
When I had given upon myself
And said Lord I cant do it anymore
You didn't set me on a shelf
And say for you I have no use for
But you took over and showed unto me
That with you at control
There was hope in your holy name
And that you with my mind and soul Would not
play a deadly game
And when I sing praises to God,
It's another way Of asking God for His aide
In my problems, that seem to rise each day
Satans hold on me seems to fade
As you take on me a new hold
And set my mind at ease
I feel a reason to be bold
As satans power leaves
I thank you Jesus my precious Lord
For in you I have encouragement
For as the saints pray in one accord
Ministering angels, to me are sent
There isn't anything or anyone
In this world so great
That can give unto me this love
Not even my human mate
But only the powers of you above

I love you Jesus, I praise you
For not giving up on me
When I didn't know what to do
I give praise and honors and glory to thee
As I do I feel a peace
Rising up with all my being
From satans power I feel a release
As though for the first time I'm seeing
That no matter how unworthy I feel
And how weak I seem to be
You will be my strength and shield
When I surrender the battles unto thee

"Signs for our own Sake"

As we start out in our Christian walk,
The Lord guides the way we feel peace and
confident, Although we know there are a lot of miles
to go
There are signs easy to follow as we pray
Whether to go fast or to go slow
There is a path to follow, straight ahead
Then there's detours we're bound to take
But always remember the blood that was shed
And it was for the purpose of our own sake
There are dangers as we all travel,
Some in front, some behind
Some to your left, some to your right
But you will always find
That you do not have to fight
The lord will fight the battles for you
As long as you do your part
He will help you in all you do
As long as you trust him with your heart
He will guide you and keep you on the right track
Just trust him and know he knows best
And you wont want to turn your back
And when you are tired, he will give you rest
Thru different ways he will talk with you
And different ways you will be fed
He will show you what you need to do
Remember he knows what lies ahead
At times he will assure you of his power
As he sees fit the request giving
In the very lowest hour

You wonder if life is worth living
As his coming is getting near
You become tired ,weary and weak
But don't stop to fear
But be more determined his will to seek
You will see others turning back,
When they were oh so close to being with him
But don't look back and let satan tell you
The Lord will not come
Remember no one knows when,but the father,
Not even the angels in heaven or gods only son
As we travel down the road towards our goal
The Lord is with us, right by our side
He's in control of our soul
And in us he will abide
You might say I started out, all this new to me
But we are not by ourselves alone
He will mold us into what he wants us to be
Although all he wants, is not yet to us shown
For he has to teach us obedience, truth and trust
Although we couldn't see, the purpose just then
To go thru a trial is a must
To teach us for one,
That he is our friend
And to teach us, trust is required
To get us thru each thing we face
To be pleasing, obedient and willing is what is
desired
And part of that is what is needed in this race
There are signs to guide the way
And warnings of the directions to take
And I can truly say
He chastises us for our own sake.

"As we grow"

We can stand on the mountain top, oh so high
We could spread our wings and fly
While we are up there, we can witness and pray Give
unto the lord, praises so great
We know exactly just what to say
To a sinner before it's to late
But when we go down to the valley below
We can hardly see, for the mountain so high
The sun shine is only a glow
And our wings are broken so we cant fly
We try to be strong on our own
We try not to say a word of disbelief
We try not to grumble or groan
We only pray for a mighty relief
Of this pain that we bare
We try to keep our head held high
Try to remember that there is someone who cares
We grow weary when we try and try
But when we do all we can
On our own power
All we can do is stand
And at that very hour
When we feel we cant bare anymore
There at the bottom opens a door
Then we see the purpose of it all
Why we had to be there
And we begin upon Jesus to call
For He is the one who does care
We learn from experiences of valleys below Although
sometimes we do not understand

That's the way he plans it so we can grow
To be a better woman or man
The Lord is in control of it all
Where we will have to go
If we shall stand or if we will fall
Unto us he will lovingly show
For he knows what it takes to make us strong
What he has to do
To teach us right from wrong
He knows when, where and who
And what is needed in each step we take
For all of us, he did make
So stand tall and rebuke satan in everything he tries
For Jesus is standing over us in love
And we are guarded by the angels above
That surround and encamp about us
And protect us from satans power
Each and everyday, every second,
Minute and hour
So trust in Jesus, with all your might
And don't lay back, but put up a fight
For Jesus so humbly guards us with love
As he prepares a place for us above
He's standing at the right hand of the throne
Interceding for each and everyone
To the one who created all heaven
And earth, moon, stars and the Son
The Son who he sent to die on the cross
So you and I would not be lost
The one who His blood was shed
And arose on the 3rd day from the dead
The father above took him to be with him

In heaven so we could see
That thru His Son we could be set free
Be free in Jesus name
And trust and confide in him
And your life will never be the same
As you are washed of all your sin
It took a cross, an old rugged tree
To show us his wonderous love
Trust in Jesus and you can be
Chosen to live in eternity above

"No Words for Tears"

The days seem so long
As they turn into weeks, months even years
The pain just won't go away
Nor will courage conquer my fears
I feel I'm alone without any hope
I feel I can no longer with life cope
My heart pulls me one way
My flesh says no go here
I can't decide how, why or where
I don't know or seem to really care
But deep in my heart I feel
A hint of relief within
I know the savior whom I once knew
Can cleanse me of all my sin.
Sometimes there are no words
To our deepest prayers from within
But Jesus sees our hearts
And cleanses us from where we are or have been
Although there is sometimes silence
There's a peace that these prayers God hears
From the heart deep within
This gentle flow of tears
The tears that speak silent words
That weakness from pain bring
The tears that speak silent tears
That my flesh cannot sing
Although the Peace the joy can't seem to come
Just now to the surface appear
I still believe and know my Lord hears every tear
For every angel God chose to take to be with him
He prepared them for His presence so sweet
He welcomed them with open arms

As the Heavenly Savior they did meet
He gave them angels to guide them home
And greeted them with a smile
He wiped away all the tears
And calmed all of the fear
My soul cries out to you Dear Lord
For all those lost in sin
I pick up my shield and sword souls for You I will win
Thru your word and with your presence sure
I step out in faith and love
Lord please make my heart pure as white
As the whitest dove
My heart needs to see the oppressed set free
The depressed, the ones who have lost their way
So prayers are said down on my knees
Lord help them thru their day
Send me and guide me to all those who wait
On someone to be sent to them
Lord touch them.
Heal and set free before its to late
Break those chains of sin
Use me Lord in any way that is pleasing to you
To reach the ones in need
Help me in all I do
Help me to in their hearts plant a seed
That it may grow and produce fruit of love and work
Within their heart so true
That it may make them look above
And realize who You are and what You do
I'm Gods best

"Joy peace and happiness"

Joy peace and happiness, are all sent from God above
From a loving savior, so full of love
He made the mountains, the streams and the hills
Every tree and flower, the clover in the fields
He made the oceans, the birds as they sing
He made the prayer bells in heaven to ring
He made the moon, stars and the sun
And each planet so fair
All of this he made for us to share
He made the trees that was Calvary's cross
He made the grass, the bark and the moss
That covered the tree that was used on Calvary's hill
To pay the cost of the sinners bill
A ransom was made with the blood that was shed
For all of us, even for the dead
And while in the tomb those two days
He went down into hell, the bible says
He brought forth the dead to the father above
Through all this he went through to show is love
And on the third day he arose
He walked and talked to all of those
Who believed he was dead
Because of the blood that was shed
He descended to heaven to be seated
At the right hand of the father,
Satan was defeated
And now dear sinner, He's calling you
To decide now what you are going to do
He's patiently, tenderly and kindly awaiting
So make up your mind and stop debating

For Jesus took all of our sin
Upon his shoulders way back then
And all you have to do, is ask and receive
Forgiveness and then to believe
My Lord is so precious, so true to me
He gave his life to set me free
Free from this world, so full of sin
And now He's standing by me, as my friend
He's shown me his kindness, mercy and grace
And I pray for him to help me finish this race
I will meet him one day, very soon
It could be tonight, morning or noon
For he is coming, I know that is true
For the bible says, what He said He would do
He told the disciples, I'm going away
To prepare a place, for you today
And I shall return to take you home to heaven above
There you will always remain in my love

"God sees the heart true"

I have many failures and many faults too
But thank God, He sees my heart within
I have many things I need to do
Starting with all my sin
I get up each morning with all good intent
But sometimes get lead astray
By all the things that from life gets sent
Then I have to stop and pray
My mind so full of all life's strife
That I sometimes get carried away
I try real hard to look at my life
And to seriously pray
So when you see me going the wrong way
And seem so distraught remind me of Jesus
And all He is, was and will be
Pray I do what I was taught
And that my eyes will be open to see
That Jesus knows perfect, we will never be
That we are human and sometimes can't see
What we should do
But when we bow down on our knee
God sees our heart true.

I hope and pray something in this book will help you. It may not be perfect in the way I word it or it may not be perfect of no mistakes in grammar or punctuation, etc but what matters is that "Matters of the Heart" is put into writing.

Look for upcoming books:
Children's stories
Anthology with short stories
Healing in His arms
Book of Poetry

Check out my daughters books at www.booksbyashlea.webs.com or on facebook www.facebook.com/ashleaburnsauthor

Also my daughters publishing company Faith by Grace Publishing. www.faithbygracepublishing.com

www.ingramcontent.com/pod-product-compliance
Lightning Source LLC
Chambersburg PA
CBHW051044030426
42339CB00006B/196